FOLK DESIGNS FROM THE CAUCASUS

FOR WEAVING AND NEEDLEWORK

by

Lyatif Kerimov

DOVER PUBLICATIONS, INC.

NEW YORK

PUBLISHER'S NOTE

One of the world's great weaving traditions has been preserved in Azerbaijan, a "republic" of the Soviet Union that borders on Iran. The wealth of motifs still actively used today by Azerbaijani weavers has been drawn from many Asiatic and even ancient East European sources. The outstanding skill and imagination evident in Azerbaijani carpets were already prized in Western Europe in the fifteenth century.

In 1961 the native scholar Lyatif Kerimov published hundreds of Azerbaijani motifs in clear diagrammatic form. The present volume includes most of these motifs, arranged in the order that Professor Kerimov assigned, and identified by the local names that he supplied (translated into English). The size of the designs has not been reduced.

The easily legible mesh grids make these designs immediately usable not only for weaving, but also for needlework of all kinds. The section on border elements alone (pages 87 through 120) contains well over a hundred designs that can be transferred directly into colorful and unusual belts, headbands and edgings.

Published in Canada by General Publishing Company, Ltd., 30 Lesmill Road, Don Mills, Toronto, Ontario.
Published in the United Kingdom by Constable and Company, Ltd., 10 Orange Street, London WC 2.

Folk Designs from the Caucasus for Weaving and Needlework, first published by Dover Publications, Inc., in 1974, is a selection of designs from Volume I (1961) of the work *Azerbaidzhanskii kovyor* [The Azerbaijani Carpet], published by the Akademiya Nauk Azerbaidzhanskoi SSR [Academy of Sciences of the Azerbaijani S.S.R.], Baku–Leningrad, with text in Azerbaijani and Russian.
The Publisher's Note, table of contents and captions in the present volume are based on the text of the original publication.

International Standard Book Number: 0-486-23014-7
Library of Congress Catalog Card Number: 73-80558

Manufactured in the United States of America
Dover Publications, Inc.
180 Varick Street
New York, N.Y. 10014

CONTENTS

ELEMENTS OF THE CENTRAL FIELD OF THE CARPET (pages 1–86)

FILLING AND
AUXILIARY ELEMENTS
(1–60)

Human Beings: 1, 2

Animals: 2–10

Everyday Objects: 11–19

Geometric Forms (19–42)
Stepped: 19–21. Squares and Rectangles: 22–24. Polygons: 25–28. Hooked: 29–34. Toothed: 35, 36. Fringed: 37. Circular: 38. Eight-pointed Stars: 39. Miscellaneous: 40–42.

Plant Forms (43–60)
Rectilinear: 43–53. Curvilinear: 54–60.

BASIC ELEMENTS
(60–86)

"Buta": 60–63

"Ketebe": 63–67

"Maternal Flowers": 66–76

"Gyoli" or "Khoncha": 77–83

"Gubpa": 84–86

BORDER ELEMENTS (87–120)

From Pileless Carpets: 87, 88

"Mouse's Teeth": 88

"Inner Border": 89–94

"Galloons": 95–98

"Small Borders": 99–107

"Central Borders": 107–120

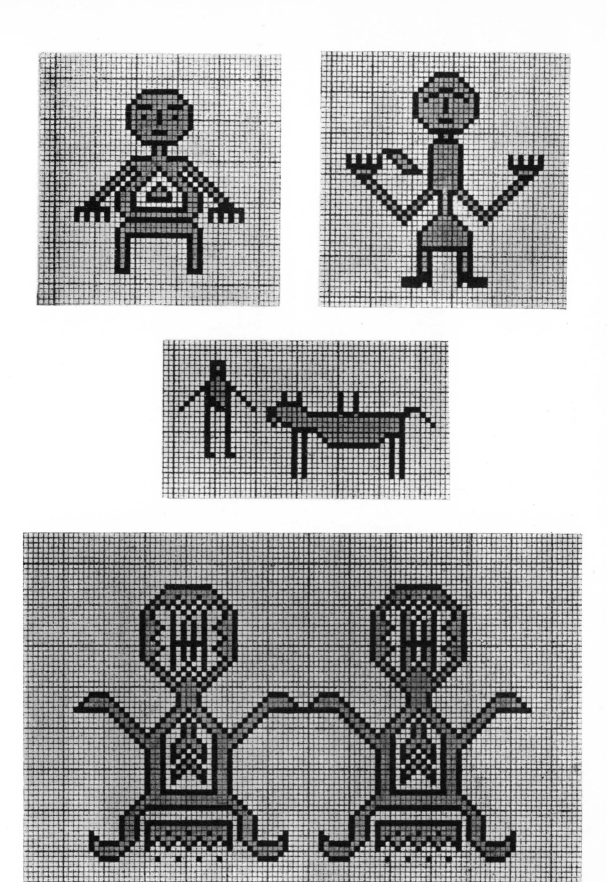

Human beings.

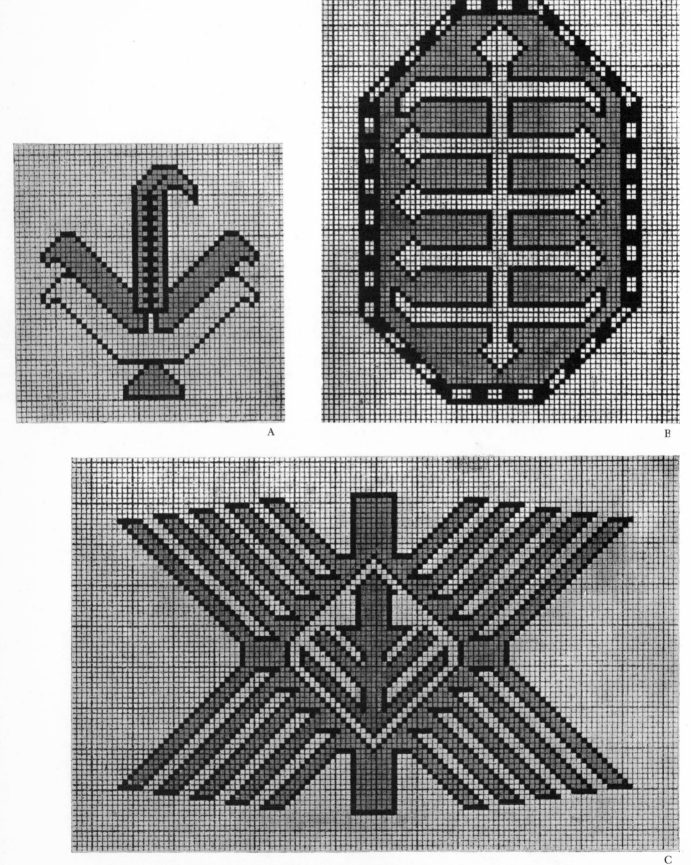

A: Bird-like motif known as "buta." B: Human being. C: Butterfly.

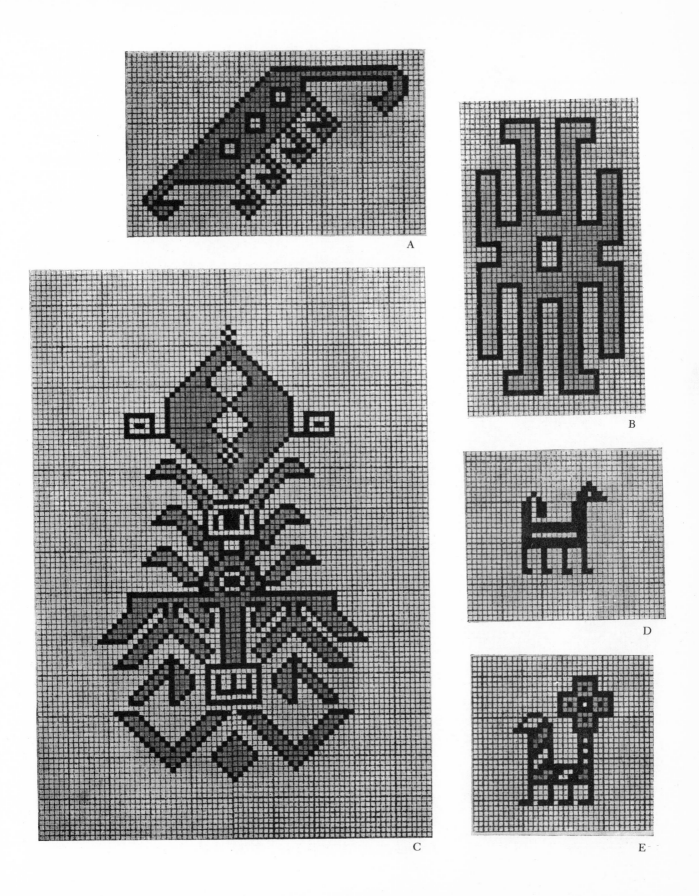

A, B, C, E: Animals, real and mythical. D: Dog.

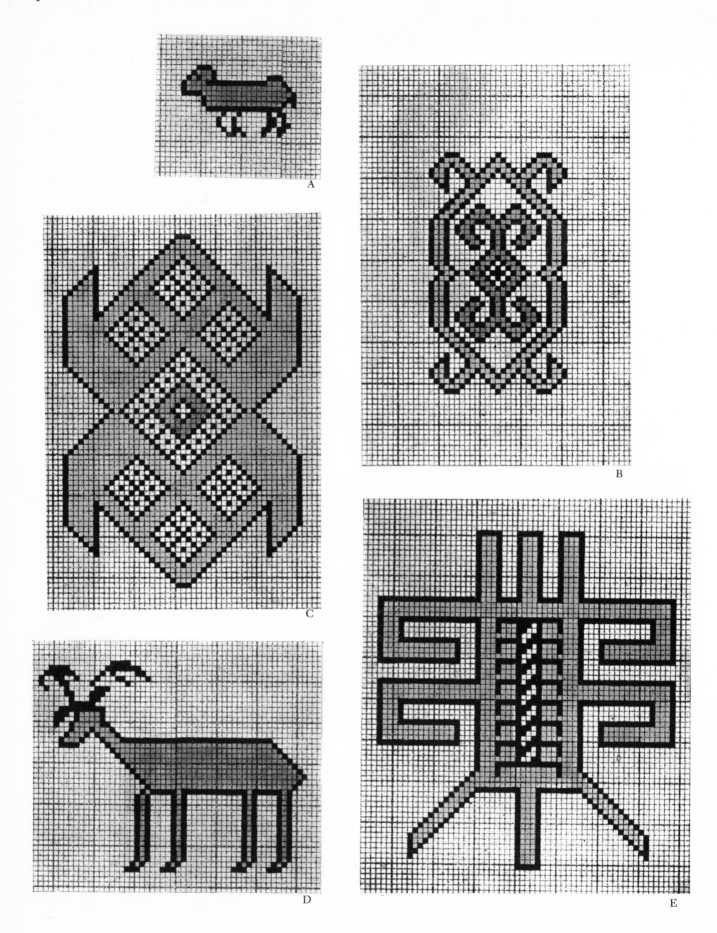

A: Sheep. B, C: Tortoises. D: Ram. E: Frog.

A: Bird. B: Camel caravan. C, D: Chamois. E: Deer.

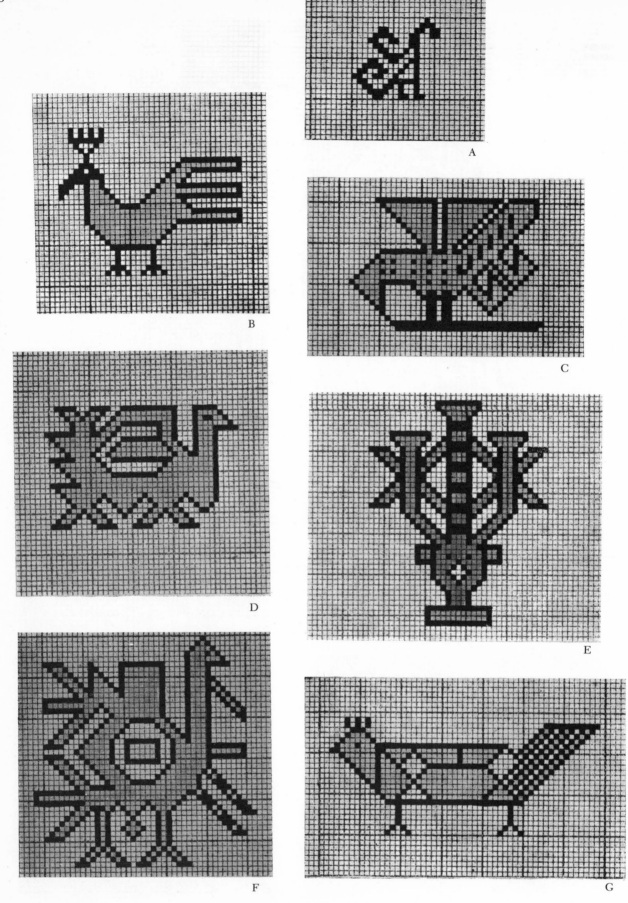

A: Bird. B: Rooster. C: Kite (bird). D: Bird (turkey?). E: Head of an animal. F: Turkey.
G: Partridge.

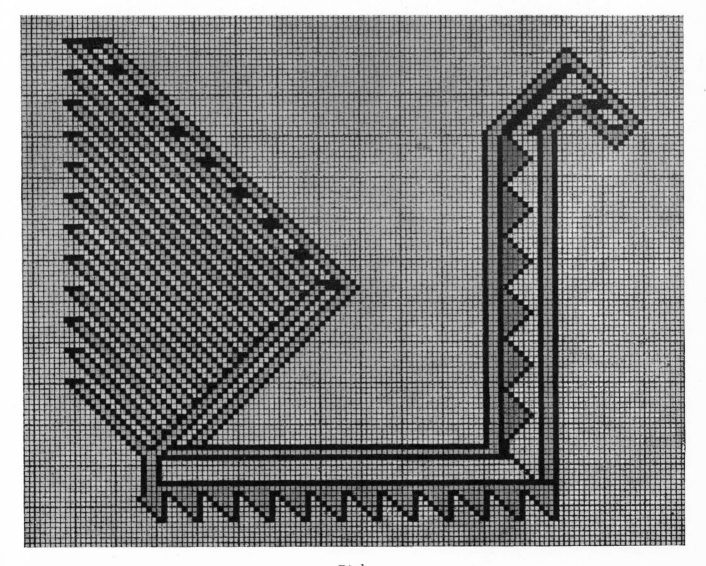

Birds.

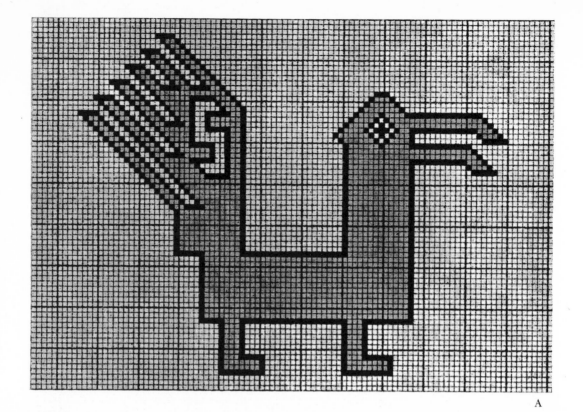

A: Turkey. B: Bat (?).

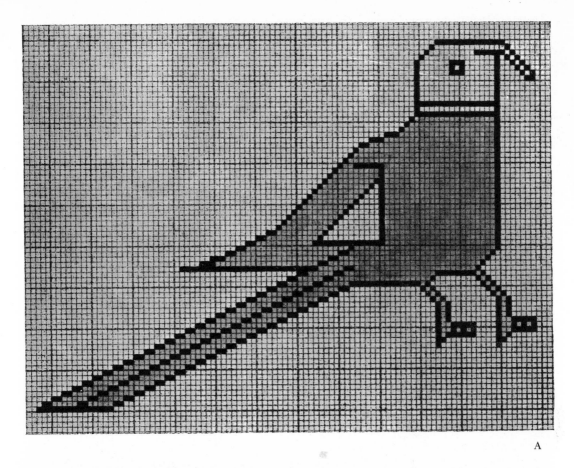

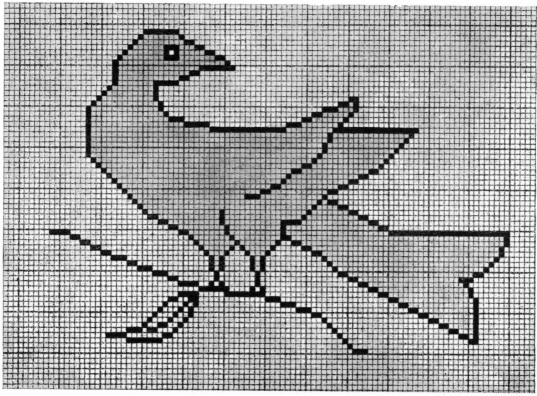

A: Parrot. B: Nightingale.

A

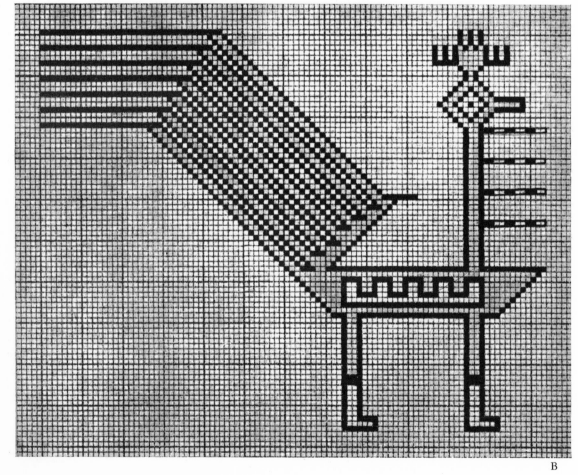

B

A: Paired animals. B: Bird.

A, B: Threshing boards. C: Axe head.

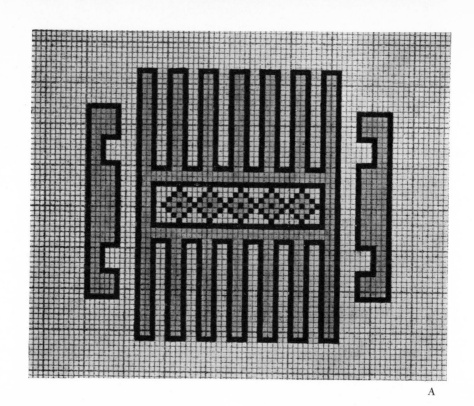

A

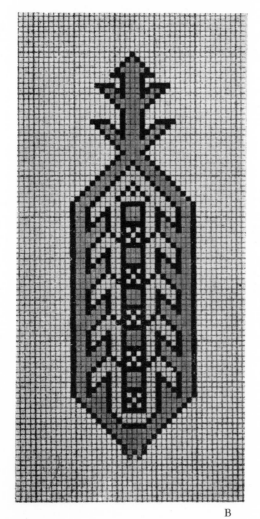

B

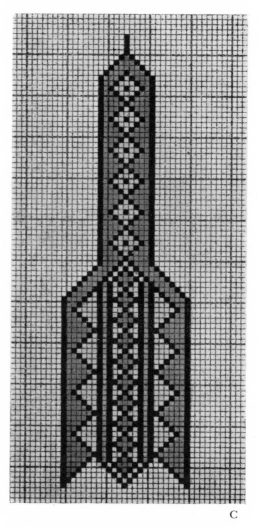

C

A: Comb. B, C: Brushes.

A, E: "Mokhur" (small flat pieces of clay from a Muslim holy site, used while praying).
B: Shirt. C: Flower or brooch. D: Processional torch.

A–D: Belt buckles. E–G: Earrings.

A, C, D: Earrings. B: Wheel.

A, B: Ablution vessels. C: Ear of grain. D: Iron spatula for working dough, or threshing board.

A: Candlestick (?). B: Hanging lamp. C: "Paw."

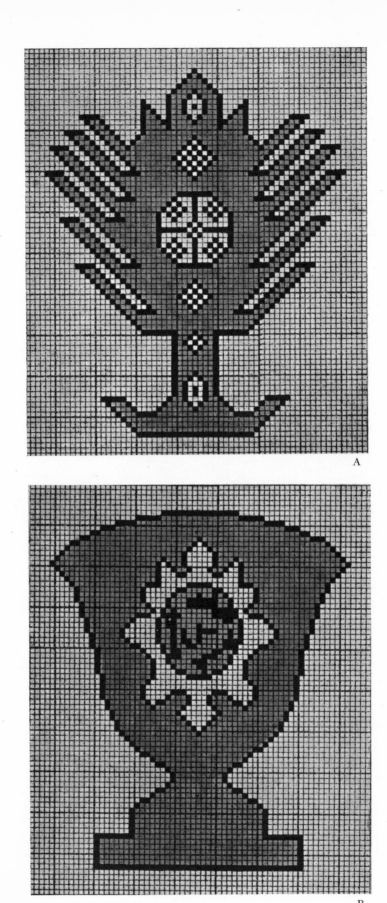

A: Candlestick. B: Vase.

A, B: Stepped motifs. C: Throne.

Stepped motifs.

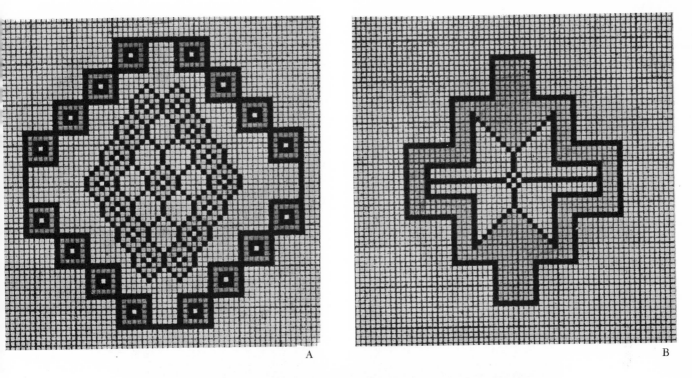

Stepped motifs (A is known as "ornamented bread loaf," C as "quilted jacket").

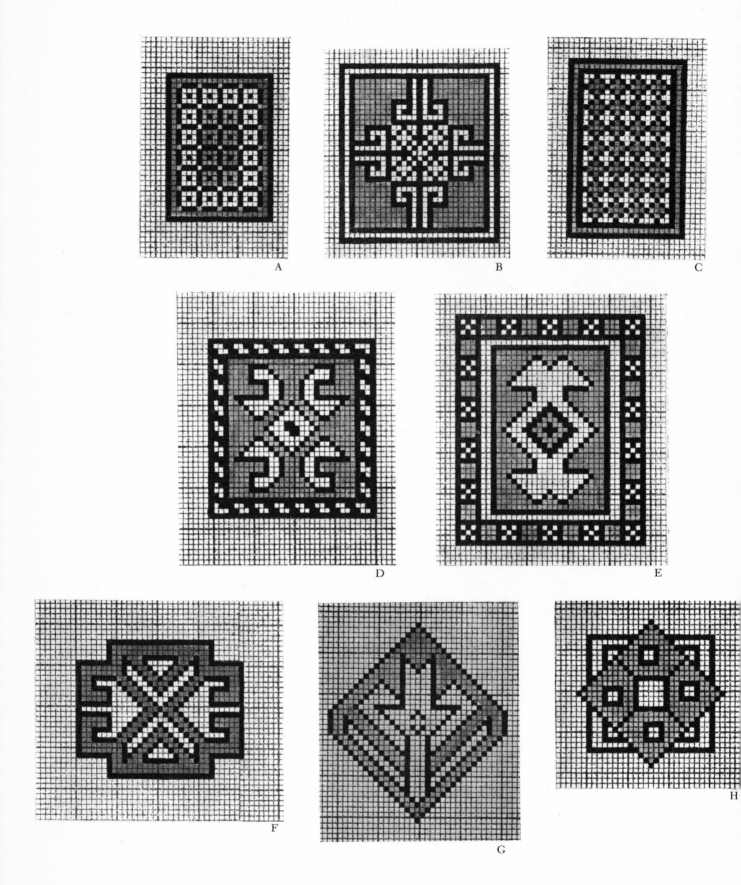

Squares and rectangles (A and C are known as "window," F as "tray").

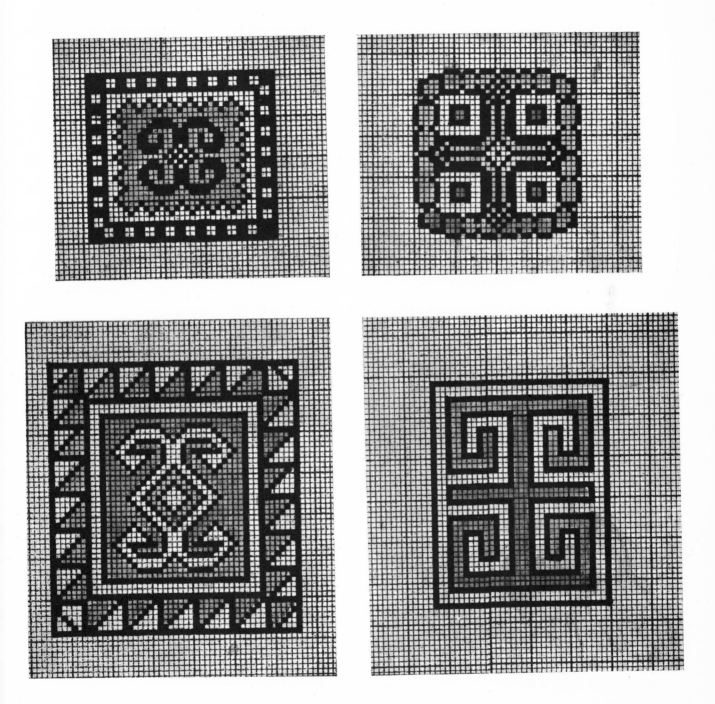

Squares and rectangles.

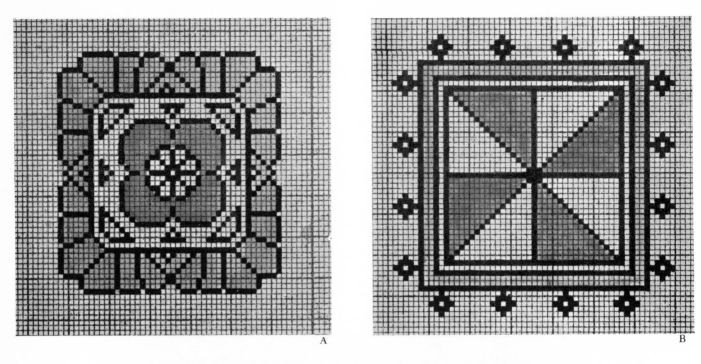

Squares and rectangles (A is known as "saucer," B as "flower with galloons," C as "majolica").

Polygons (A is known as "cradle," B as "jug," C as "mirror," D as "brick").

Polygons (C is known as "dish," E as "majolica apple").

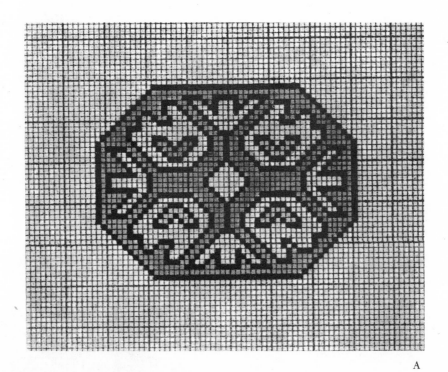

A

B

C

Polygons (B is known as "paired bows," C as "grave").

Polygons (A is known as "small round loaf," B as "curl," C as "spindle part," D as "glazed brick," E as "claw").

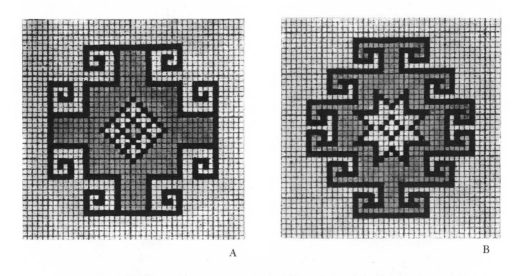

A

B

C

Hooked motifs (A is known as "claw," B as "sloe flower").

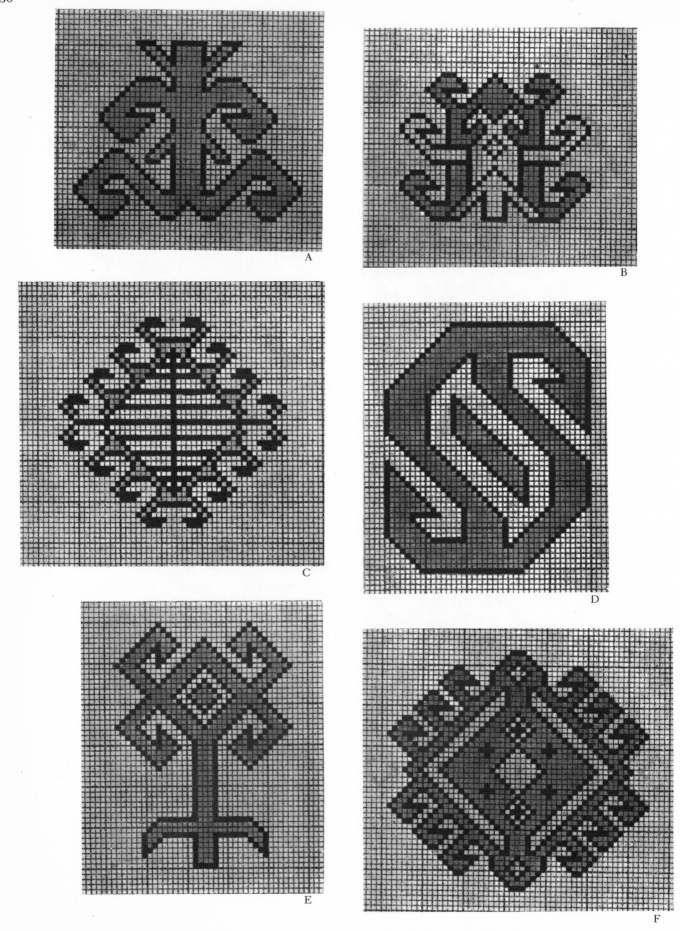

Hooked motifs (A is known as "tree," B as "crayfish," D as "curl," E as "target").

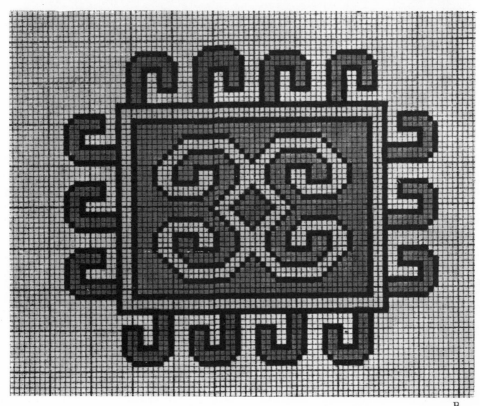

Hooked motifs (A is known as "animal").

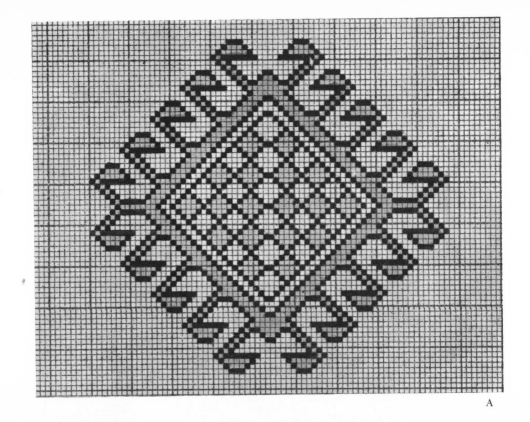

A

B

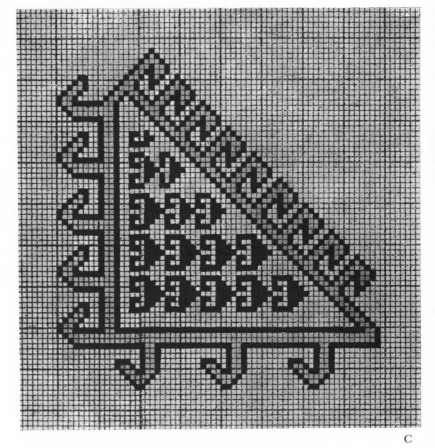

C

Hooked motifs (A is known as "animal," B as "candlestick," C as "brazier").

Hooked motifs (A and C are known as "bunch of grapes").

Hooked motif known as "shawl."

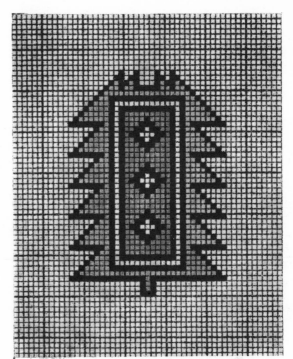

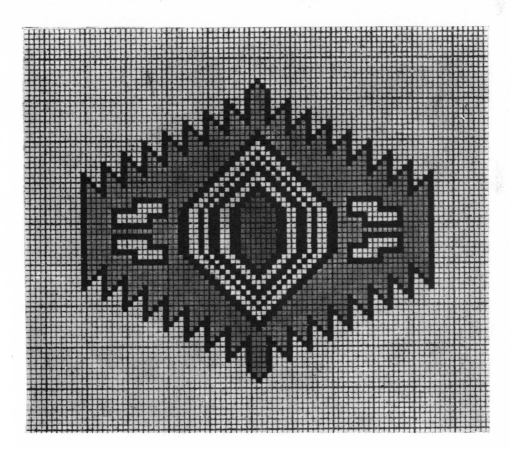

Toothed motifs.

Toothed motifs (B is known as "man with bow and arrows," C as "balcony railing," D as "flower").

Fringed motifs (A and B are known as "fence," D as "nut," E as "fan," F as "saw").

A B C D E F

Circular motifs (A and C are known as "apple," B as "vine leaf," D and E as "cake").

Eight-pointed stars (C is known as "wheel").

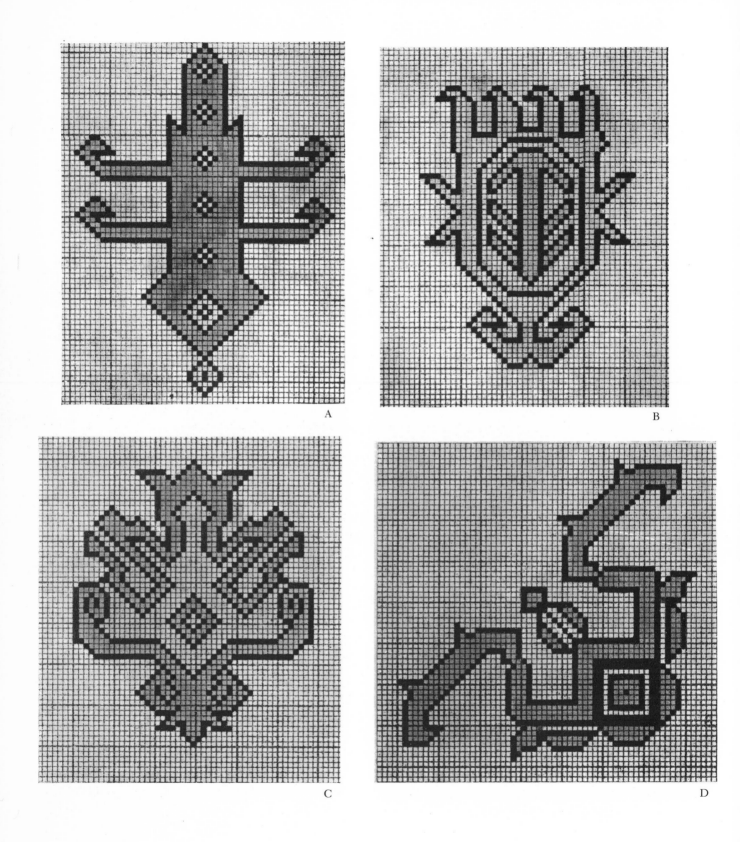

Miscellaneous geometric forms (B is known as "hand," D as "man's armband").

Miscellaneous geometric forms (A is known as "sumac flower").

Miscellaneous geometric forms.

A, B, F, I: Plant forms. C: Poppy. D, E: Cotton boll. G: Oak. H: Leaf.

44

A: Twig. B: Plant form. C, F: Steppe grass. D, E: Flowers.

A, E: Twig. B: Nut. C: Plant form. D, F: Flowers.

A, B: Plant forms. C: Oak leaf. D: Oak. E: Leaf. F: Twig.

A: Grapevine. B: Twig. C: Opening bud. D: Nut.

A, D: Leaves. B: Pomegranate. C: Apple.

A: Cotton boll. B: Plant form. C: Pomegranate flower. D: Starwort.

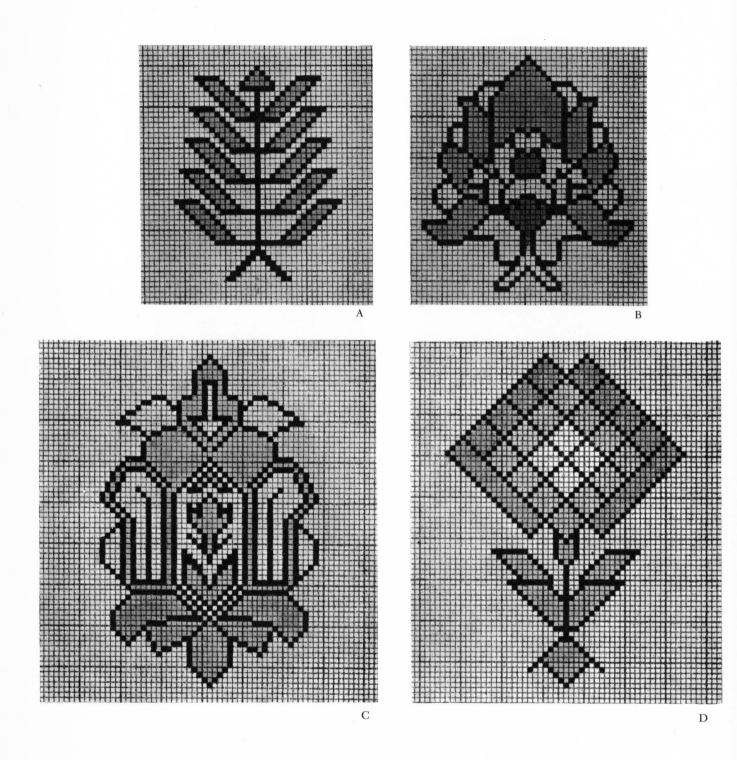

A: Branch. B: Shepherd's purse (flower). C: Bouquet. D: Plant form.

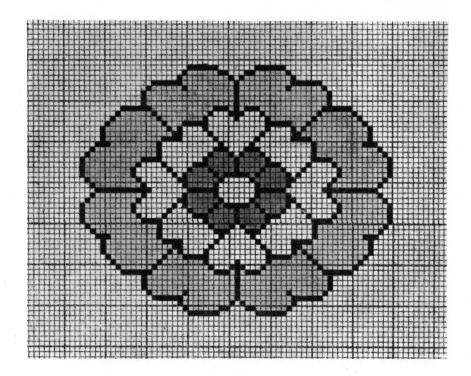

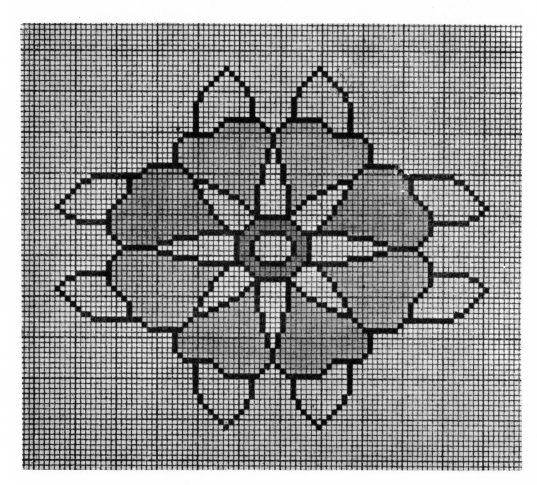

Flowers.

A: Flower. B: Pomegranate flower.

A

B

A: Flower. B: Pumpkin.

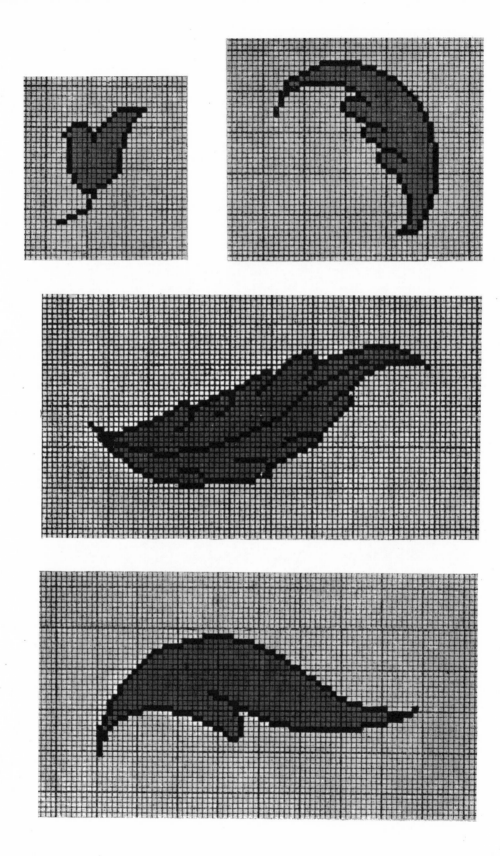

Leaves.

A: Poppy. B, C, F, G: Plant forms. D, I: Oak. E: Bean leaf. H: Alfalfa.

Flowers.

Flowers.

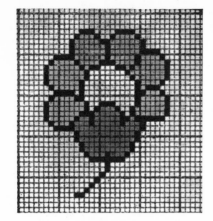

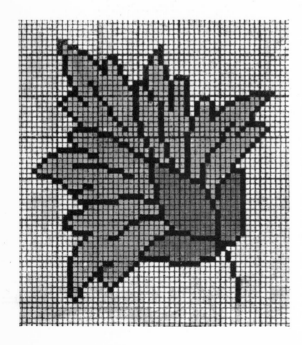

Flowers.

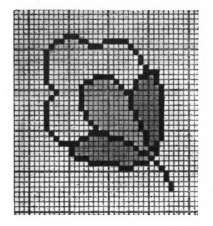

Flowers.

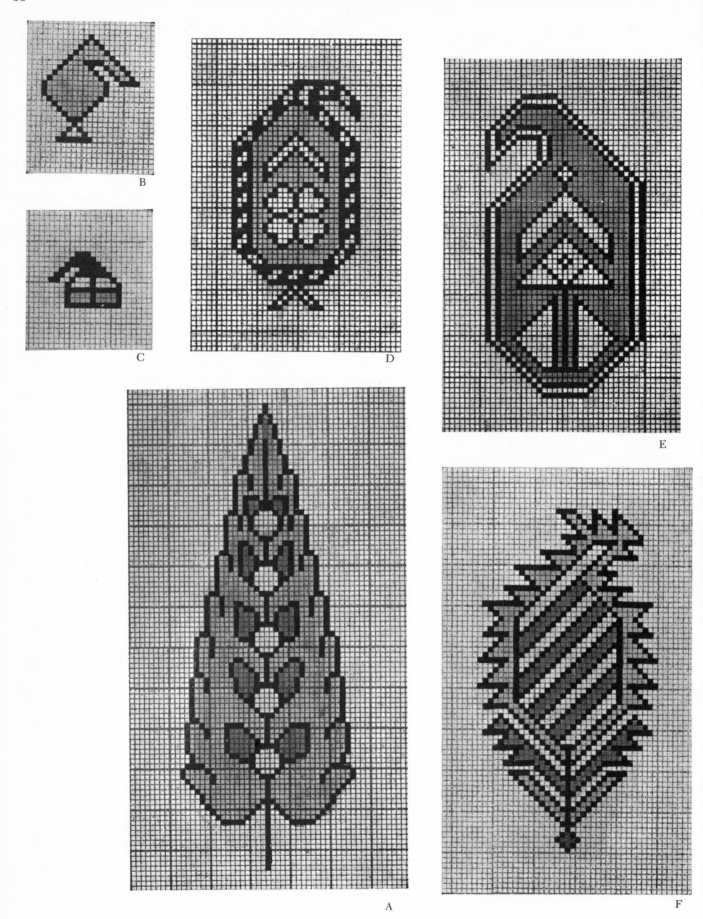

A: Poplar. B–F: "Buta" (motif of uncertain origin, perhaps representing a flame).

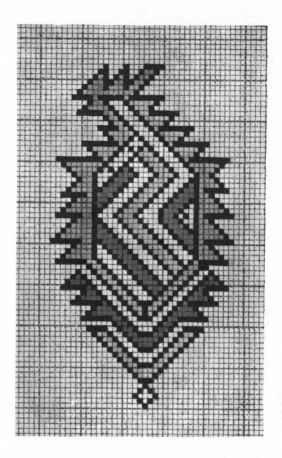

"Buta."

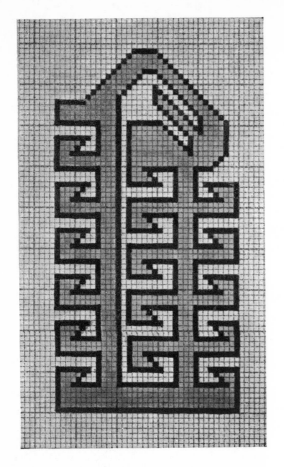

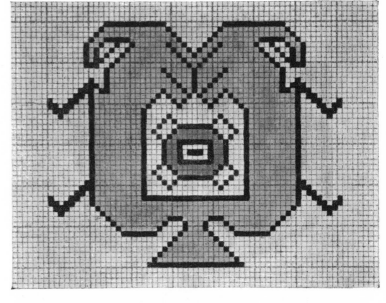

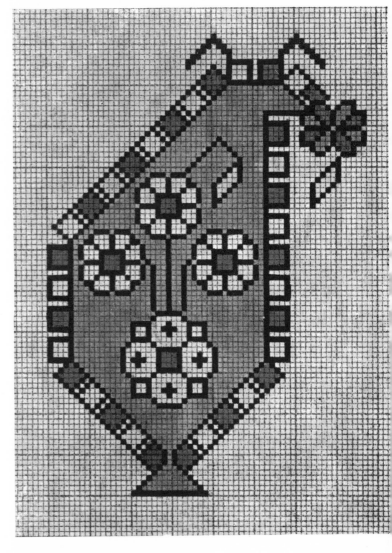

"Buta."

A, B: "Buta." C–E: "Ketebe" (motif whose name suggests a lettered frieze).

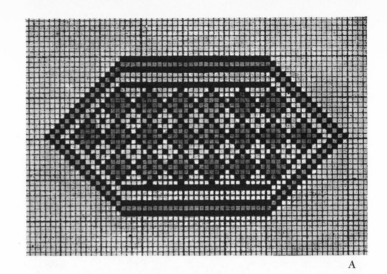

A

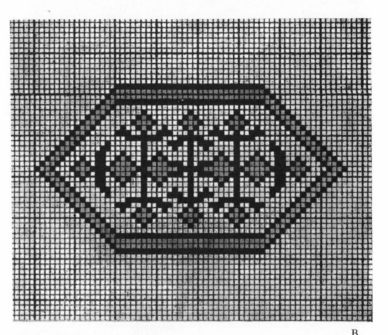

B

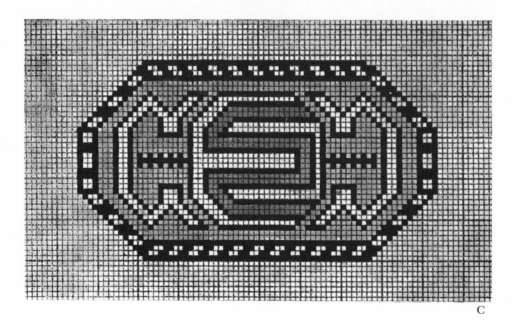

C

"Ketebe" (A is known as "cradle").

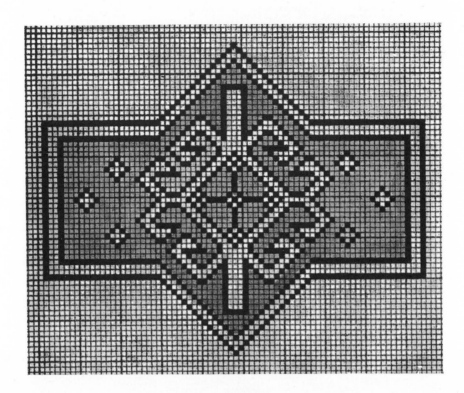

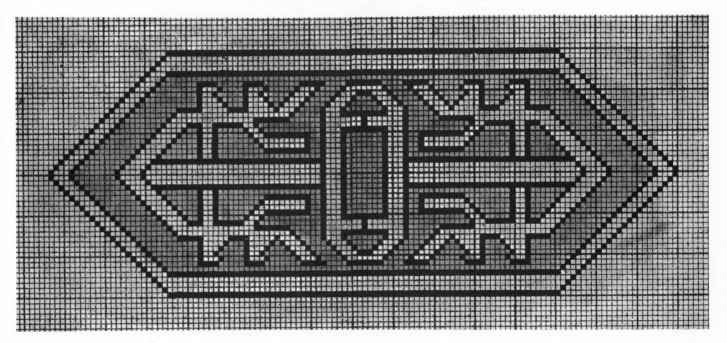

"Ketebe."

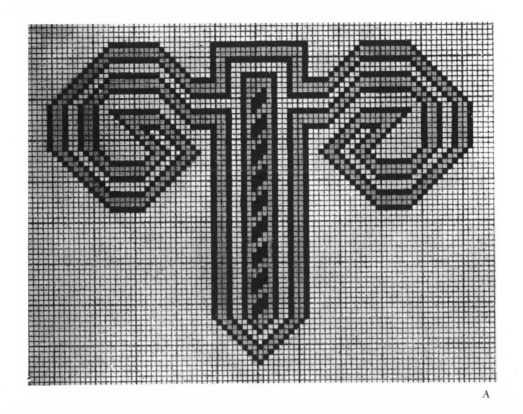

A

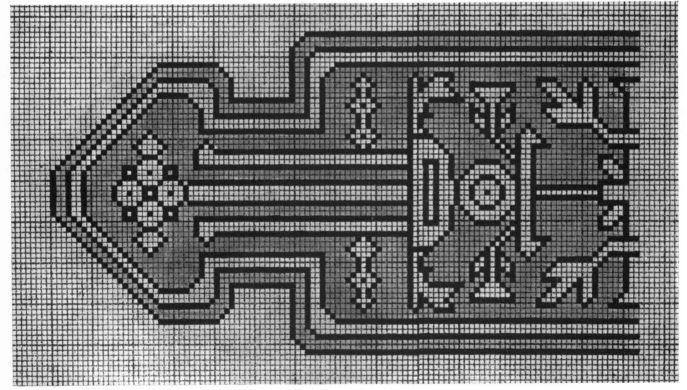

B

A: Motif known as "maternal flowers"; special type known as "scissors" (actually animal horns?). B: "Ketebe."

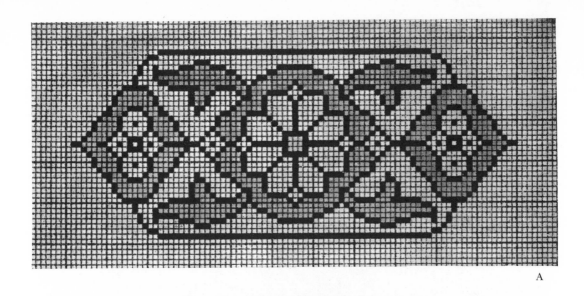

A: "Ketebe"; special type known as "wallflower." B: "Maternal flowers"; special type known as "scissors."

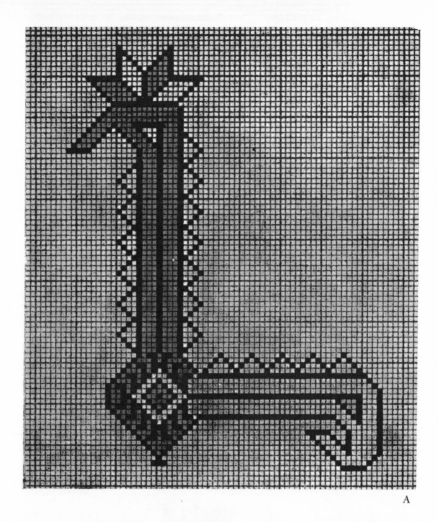

A

B

"Maternal flowers" (A is known as "tripod").

A

B

C

D

"Maternal flowers" (A is known as "white flower," B and C as "flower," D as "leaf").

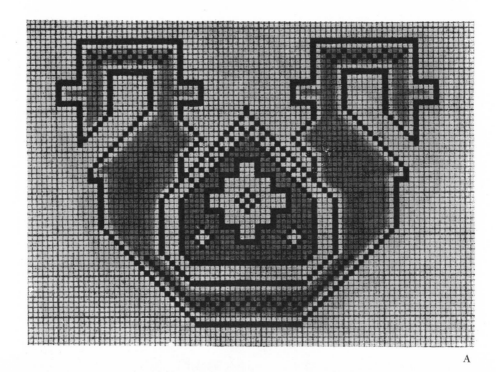

A

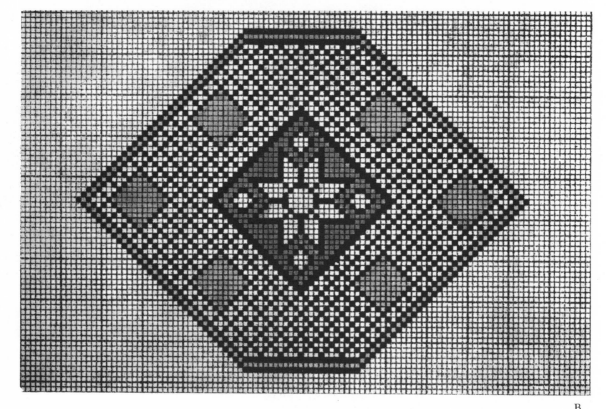

B

"Maternal flowers" (A is known as "curl").

"Maternal flowers" (A is known as "branch," B as "forest plant," C as "gate").

A

B

"Maternal flowers" (A is known as "bouquet," B as "teapot").

"Maternal flowers.

"Maternal flowers."

A

B

"Maternal flowers" (A is known as "climber," B as "bride's dowry").

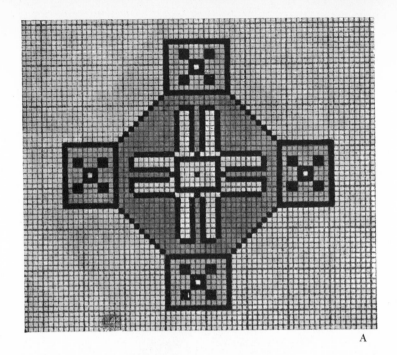

"Maternal flowers" (A is known as "wheel," B as "leaf").

A

B

Medallion-like motifs called "gyoli" or "khoncha" (A is known as "brick," B as "nail").

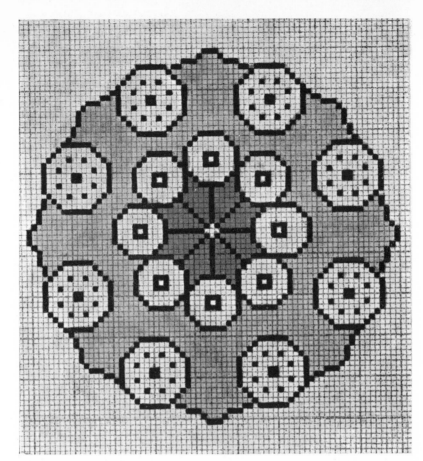

A

B

"Gyoli."

A

B

"Gyoli" (A is known as "marriage ornament," B as "camel track").

"Gyoli."

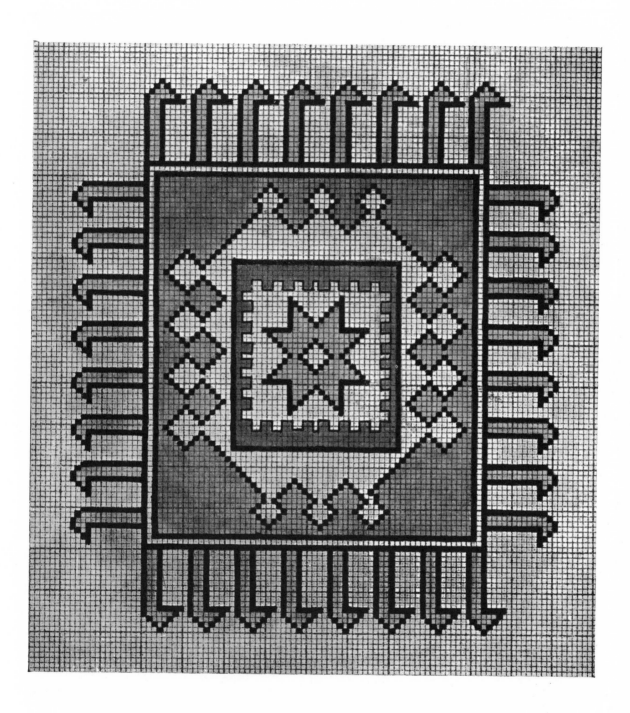

"Gyoli."

A

B

"Gyoli" (A is known as "majolica").

A

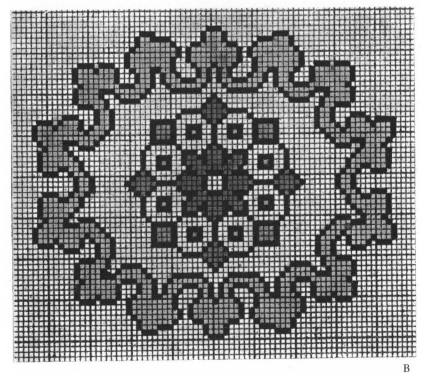

B

"Gyoli" (B is known as "circular tray").

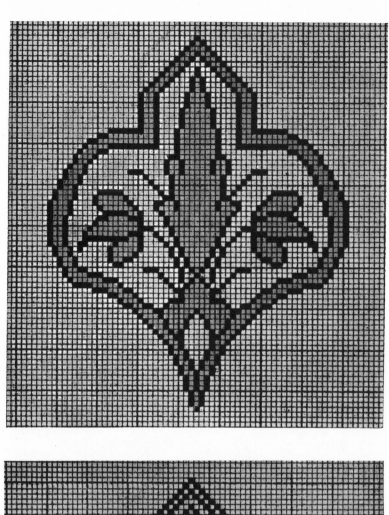

Motif called "gubpa"; special type known as "tip" or "blade."

"Gubpa."

"Gubpa"; special type known as "head of a statue."

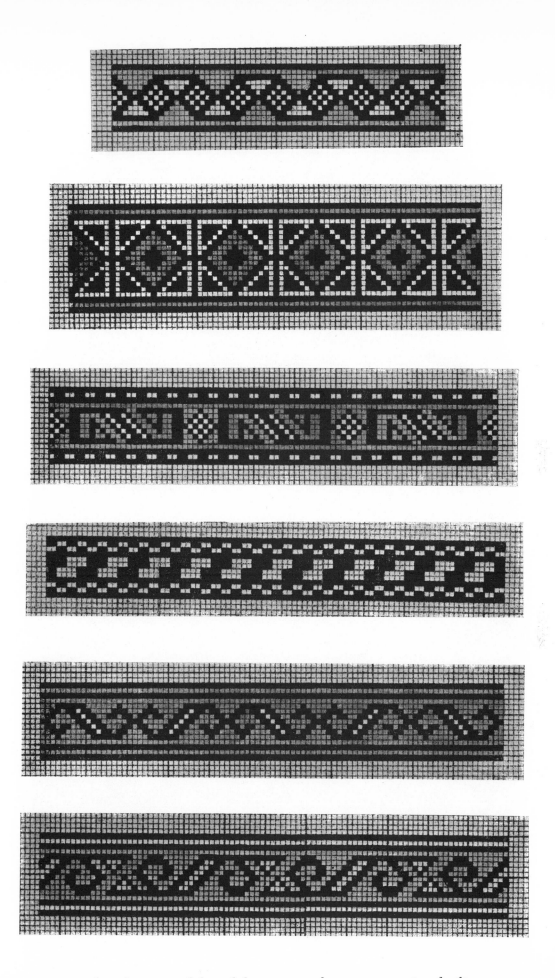

Border elements of the pileless carpets known as *verni* and *zili*.

A, B: Border elements from *verni* and *zili*. C–F: Border elements called "mouse's teeth" (C is known as "toothed," D as "curtain ornament," E as "curls," F as "chain").

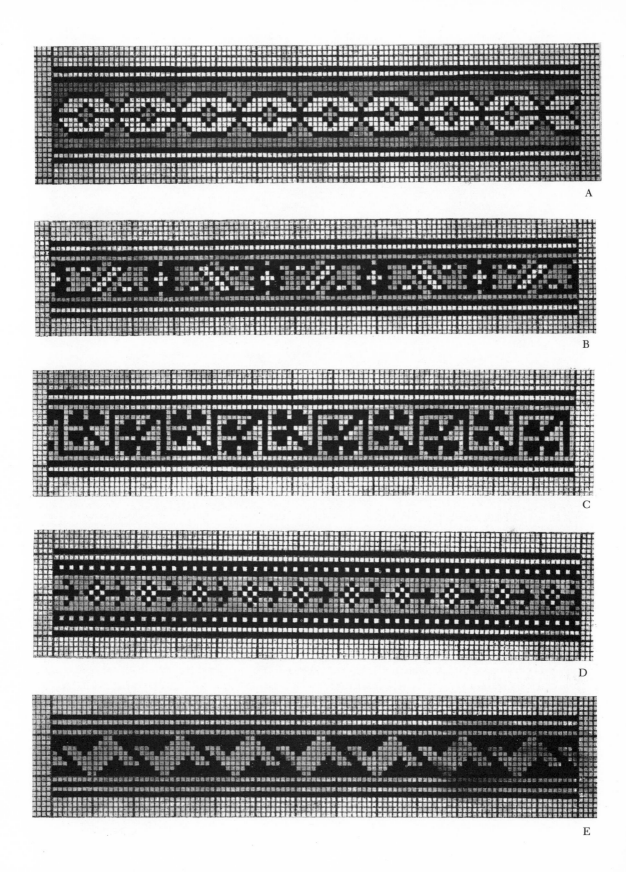

Border elements: "inner border" (B is known as "chain," C as "mallow," D as "twig,"
E as "lightning").

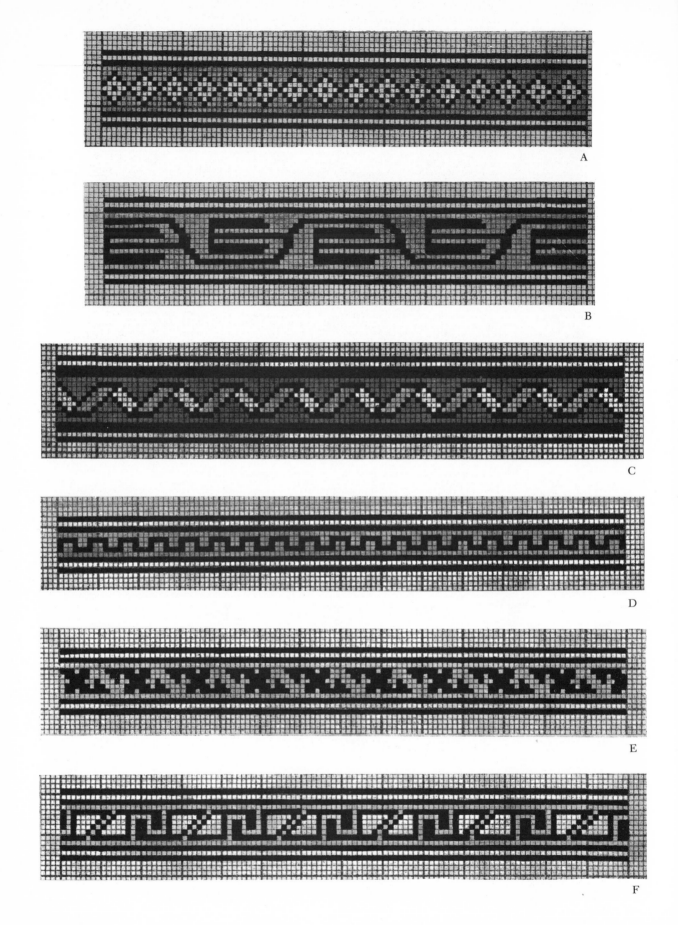

"Inner border" (A is known as "dashes," B as "hanging," C as "curls," D as "track of young animal's urine," E as "hooks," F as "paired claws").

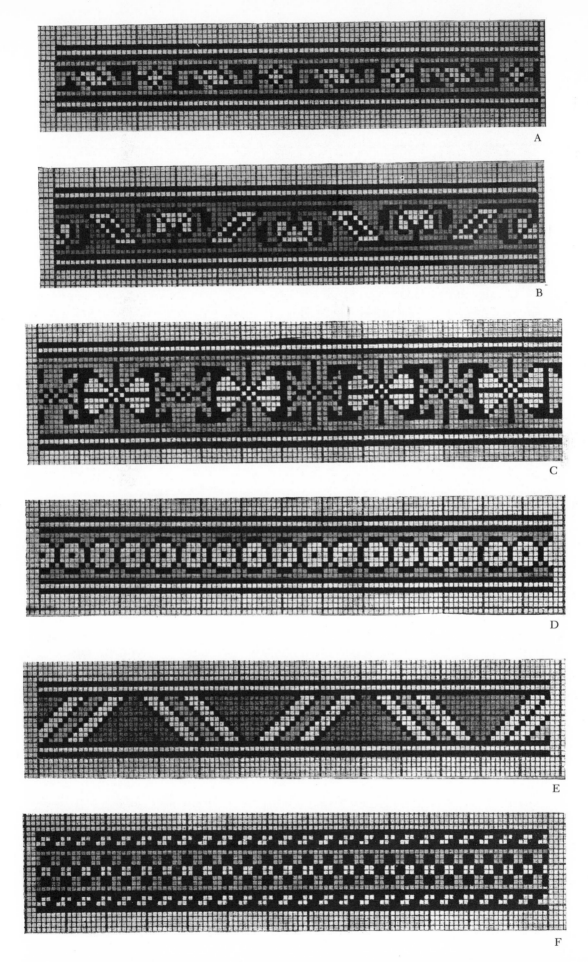

A

B

C

D

E

F

"Inner border" (A is known as "chain," D as "buttons," E and F as "curls").

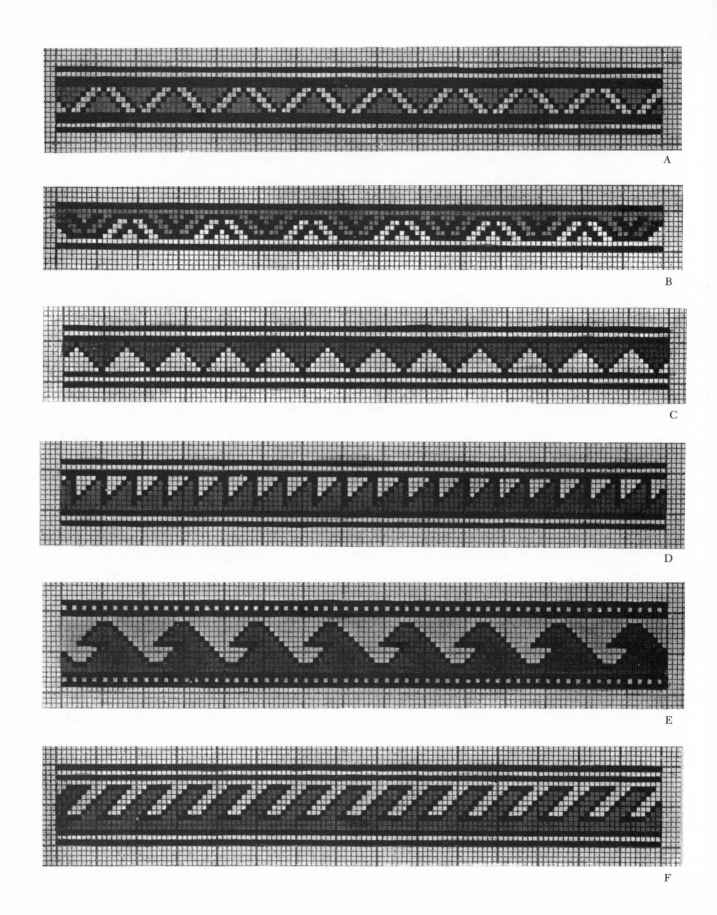

"Inner border" (C is known as "toothed," D and F as "saw," E as "animal").

"Inner border" (A is known as "hooked," B as "chains," D as "ketebe" [see Plate 63],
E as "armband").

"Inner border" (A is known as "curls," C as "curved claws," D as "branch," E as "white flowers").

Border elements: "galloons" (A is known as "chain," B as "buta" [see Plate 60]).

"Galloons" (A is known as "chain," C as "flowery," E as "apricots with twigs").

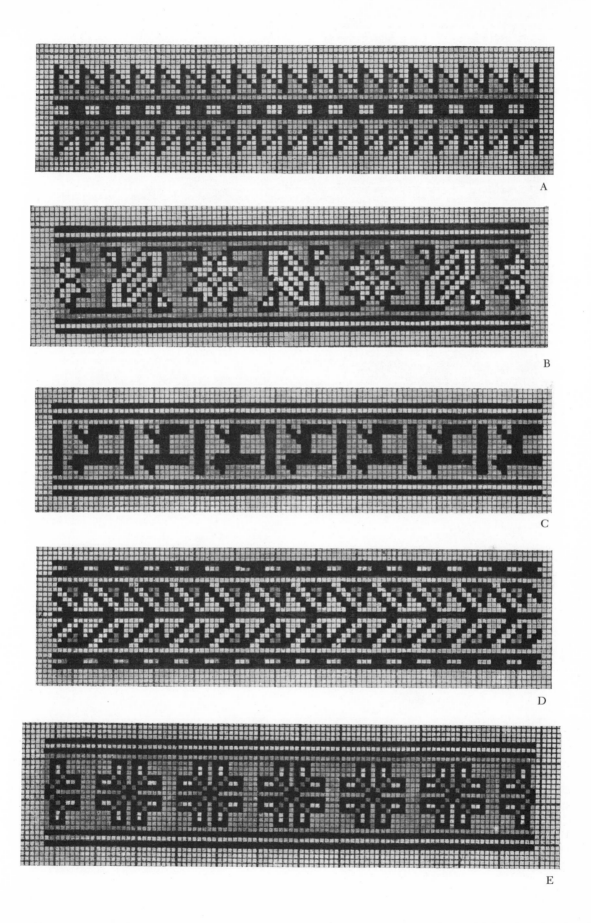

"Galloons" (A is known as "saw," B as "scissors," C as "animals," E as "quince flowers").

"Galloons" (C is known as "mullah's heads," D as "festive flowers").

Border elements : "small borders" (B is known as "twisted claws").

A

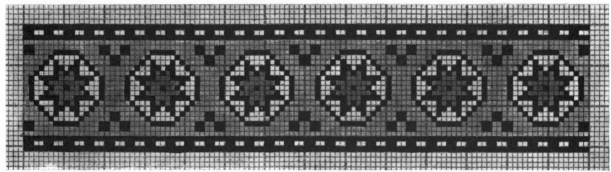

B

C

D

"Small borders" (B is known as "buttons," D as "mallow flowers").

"Small borders" (A is known as "bindweed," B as "curls," D as "paired hooks").

"Small borders" (A is known as "cotton bolls").

A

B

C

D

"Small borders (D is known as "cradles").

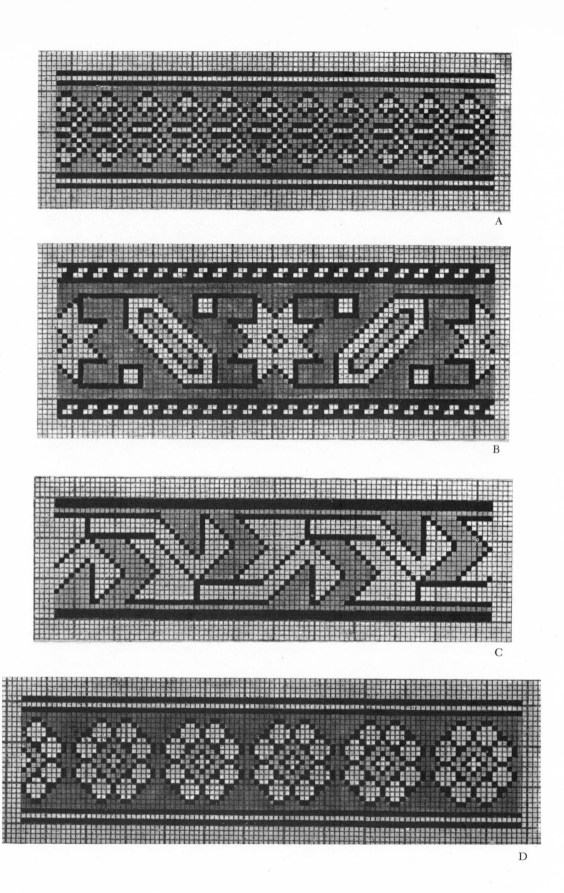

"Small borders" (A is known as "arrowheads," B as "scissors," C as "button-flowers").

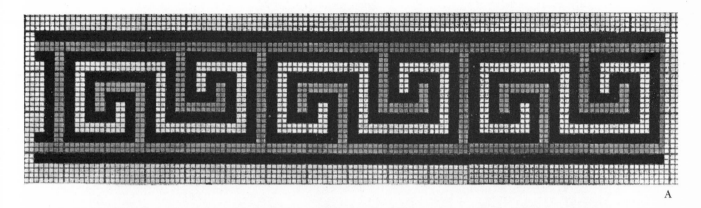

A

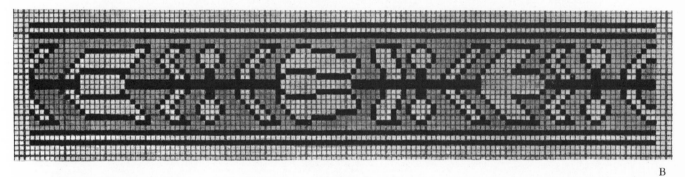

B

C

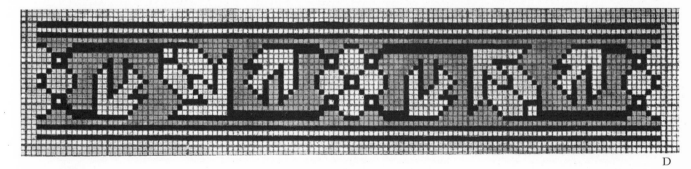

D

"Small borders" (A is known as "[firearm] cocks," C as "hearths").

"Small borders" (C is known as "medallion flowers," D as "chicken legs").

A: "Small borders" known as "[firearm] cocks." B–D: Border elements: "central borders" (B is known as "ketebe border" [see Plate 63], C as "cherries").

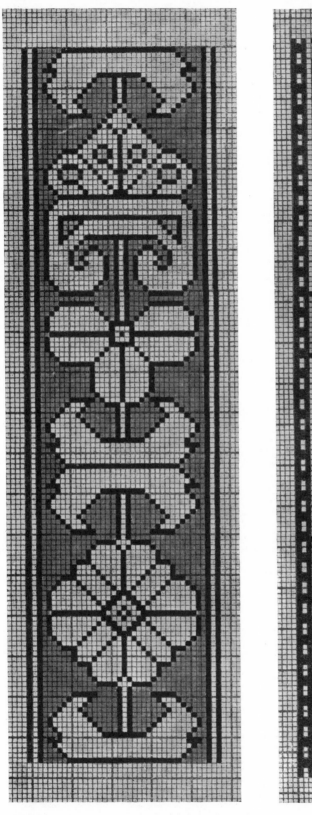

"Central borders."

"Central borders" (A is known as "candlesticks," B as "pitchforks and plows").

"Central borders" (A is known as "ancient statues").

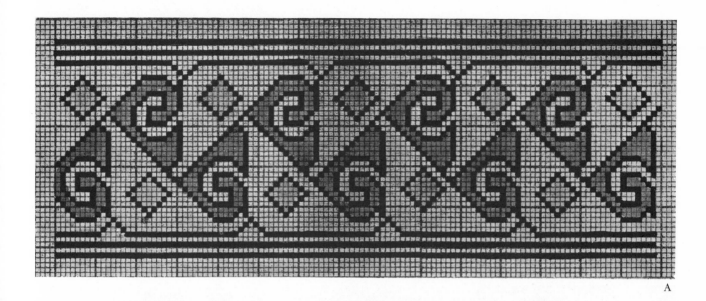

A

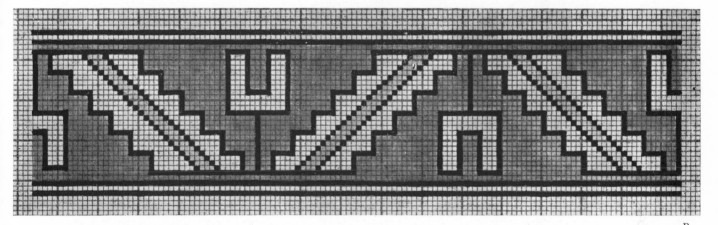

B

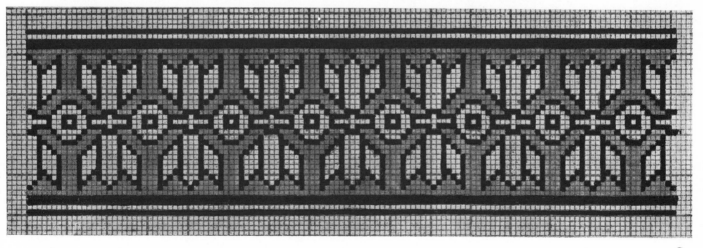

C

"Central borders" (A is known as "curly tresses," B as "torches," C as "honeycombs").

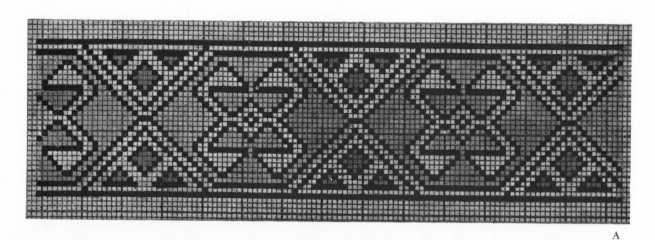

A

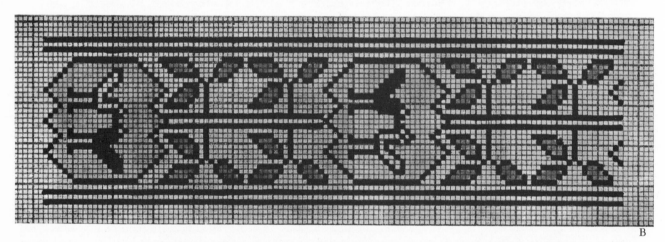

B

C

"Central borders" (B is known as "paired birds," C as "tresses").

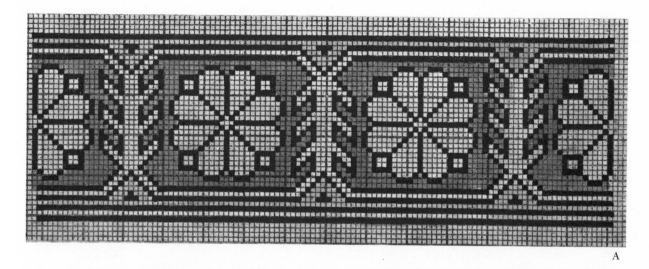

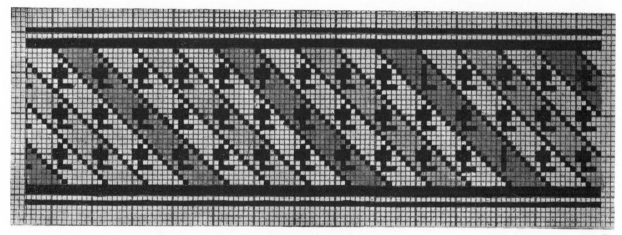

"Central borders" (C is known as "hearths").

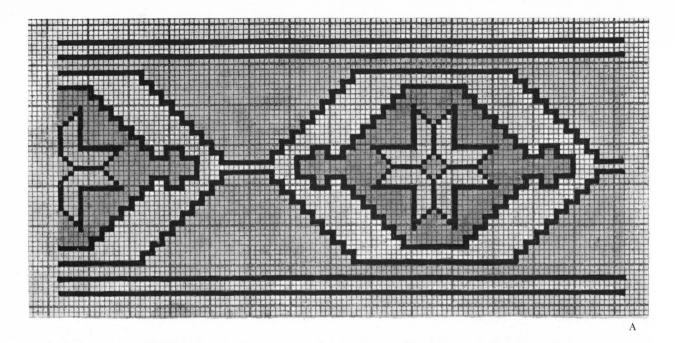

A

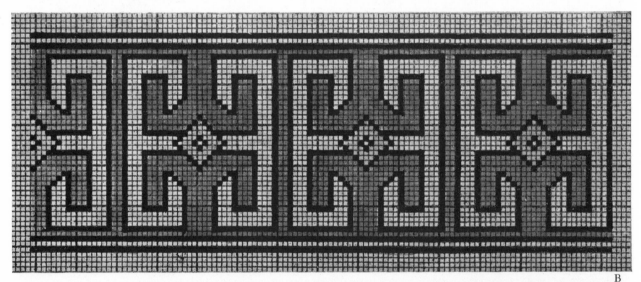

B

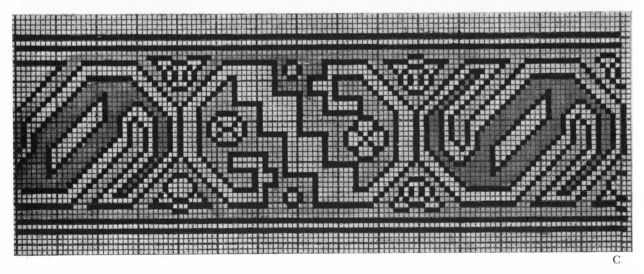

C

"Central borders" (A is known as "cradles," B as "balcony railings," C as "[firearm] cocks").

A

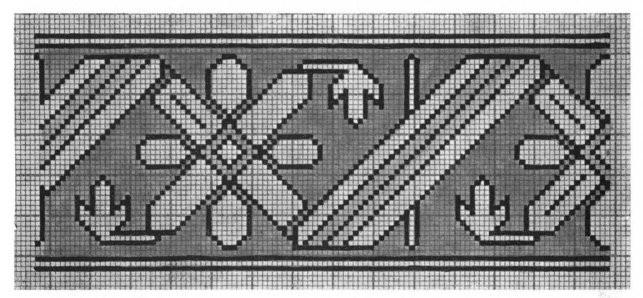

B

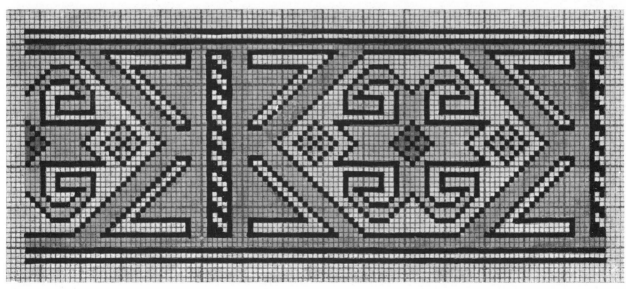

C

"Central borders" (C is known as "cradles").

"Central borders"

A

B

C

"Central borders" (A and B are known as "majolica").

A

B

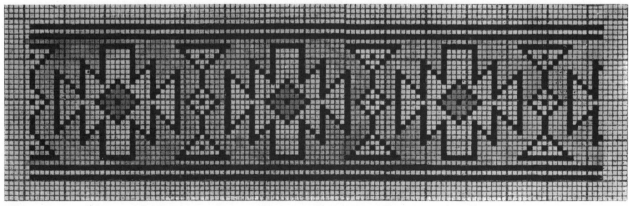

C

"Central borders" (B is known as "railing").

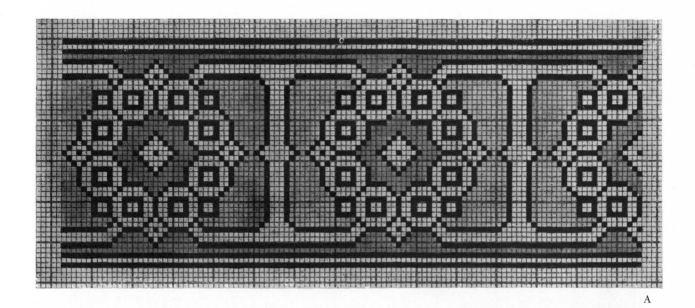

A

B

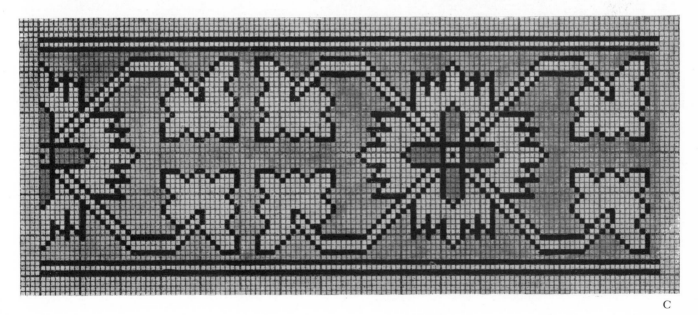

C

"Central borders" (C is known as "ringlet border").

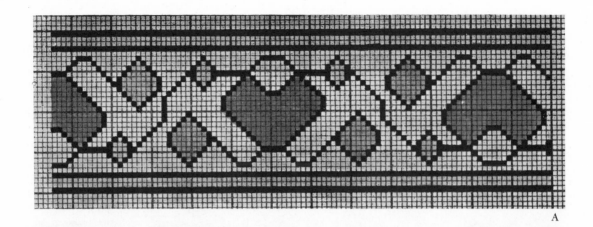

"Central borders" (C is known as "glass gallery").